THE TRUTH BEYOND
THE HUMAN

THE TRUTH BEYOND THE HUMAN

SANDOR ONISIM BERECZKI

Copyright © 2025 by Sandor Onisim Bereczki.

ISBN: 978-1-9192134-0-8

All rights reserved. No part of this publication may be reproduced, or transmitted in any form or by any means, including photocopying, recording, or other electronic or mechanical methods, without the prior written permission of the publisher.

Published by: Sandor Onisim Bereczki.

Printed in the United States of America

Contents

INTRODUCTION
The Truth Beyond the Human — vii

CHAPTER 1
Who We Are and Why We Are Here — 1

CHAPTER 2
Access to Universal Memories – Remembrance and Past Lives — 9

CHAPTER 3
Possible Futures and Destiny — 17

CHAPTER 4
Memories from Past Lives — 25

CHAPTER 5
Encounters Beyond the Veil — 35

CHAPTER 6
Memories of Power and the Lesson of Love — 43

Chapter 7
Cyclical Lives – Circles of Existence   51

Chapter 8
Prisoner or Free on Planet Earth   59

Chapter 9
Methods for Healing the Soul   67

Chapter 10
Healing the Soul   77

Chapter 11
Truths Beyond the Human   85

Epilogue
The Journey of the Soul and the Return to Love   91

Introduction

The Truth Beyond the Human

This book is not just a collection of personal experiences.

It is a sincere confession, an inner journey that traverses multiple lives, dimensions, and states of being.

I have set down these lines not to convince, but to share what has been gently revealed to me over time.

The truths within these pages do not ask for acceptance.

They only ask for an open heart.

They will enter where they are needed and will blossom when the reader's soul is ready, guided by the universal law of balance.

Chapter 1

Who We Are and Why We Are Here

Who We Are and Why We Came to Earth

I am the one who writes now. And I am also the one who reads. I am the one who listens, feels, and breathes this very moment. Because beyond appearances, beyond forms and roles, we are One. What seems to separate us – the ego, the identity, the physical body – is only a temporary veil, meant to create the illusion of individuality.

The ego prevents us from seeing this unity. But beyond it, beyond the story we tell ourselves about who we are, there exists a Single Consciousness, a Single Spirit manifested in countless forms, living diverse experiences on Earth, in other dimensions, on other planes of existence.

When the ego is truly set aside, your Spirit reconnects with the Higher Spirit – the source from which you come. In that state, truth becomes clear, and you remember who you really are. The Higher Spirit is pure, loving, and perfect in essence. To align with it means to live in harmony, to be in balance with the entire Universe.

It is fascinating that many religions speak about salvation, about rules and conditions to follow. Yet very few truly guide you to know yourself, to seek your root within your own heart, and to live truth through direct experience, not blind belief.

So I gently ask you: Who are you?

Perhaps you will answer with your name – the one given by your parents. Perhaps you will speak of your profession, of the body you inhabit. Yet beyond all of this, before you received a name, a role, a destiny, your Spirit stepped into this body. That Spirit is you. Name, education, beliefs – all of these are learned along the way. But you, the true one, are eternal and alive beyond them.

I do not ask you to believe what I write here. But I invite you, with all love, to search, to feel, and to discover. Truth is not a theory, but a living experience. Let your soul inquire, question, feel beyond words. Discover who you truly are and what gifts you carry within you – not for validation, but to offer them to the world.

Perhaps you have received religious, social, or cultural beliefs and accepted them without questioning, because that is what you were told. And that is natural. But true knowledge begins when you dare to look beyond what "is said" and listen to your heart.

This book is a guide. A calling. I have written it to accompany you in understanding the reason you came to Earth and the deeper purpose you have here: to experience, to learn, to love, and to evolve.

The Mind – Your Friend or Your Enemy

No matter what happens around you, true strength is born within. Authentic power does not mean dominating or controlling, but keeping inner peace in the midst of the storm. It is that state of profound stillness, which does not depend on outer circumstances, but on how you choose to respond to life.

This state can be cultivated by observing thoughts, by becoming aware of emotions, and by gradually quieting the mind. It is not easy to remain at peace when surrounded by restless people, disturbing energies, or tense contexts. That is why it is essential to train your attention – to draw it away from the chaos of the world into the silence of your heart. Only there, in that sacred space within you, do you find true balance.

If you focus all your attention only on material things, you cannot expect a meaningful and deeply fulfilling life. But neither are extremes the solution. True wisdom lies in harmony – between body, mind, emotions, and spirit. It is the fine dance of balance.

When someone hurts or offends you, you have the power to decide what you allow inside. You can open the door to suffering, or you can remain in the stillness of the one who knows that no word defines you. Emotions do not appear out of nowhere – they are generated by your mind, influenced by the patterns you have absorbed throughout life.

But if you look closely around, you will notice that very few people are truly happy. And the reason, most often, lies in their own mind. The mind can be a divine tool, but also a double-edged sword. It creates your emotions, your reactions, your perceptions of the world.

True happiness does not come from outside – it is revealed from within, when the mind ceases to seek and begins to serve your inner stillness.

The Mask People Wear

Behind forced smiles, carefully chosen words, and carefully constructed appearances, many people hide a painful silence. Some carry within them a gentle heart, a deep sensitivity, but choose to cover it. Why? Because too often, they have been hurt.

Thus the mask is born.

In an environment that values toughness, control, outward success, many choose – consciously or unconsciously – to build an image: colder, more distant, stronger. But this apparent strength is not authentic. It is protection. A defense mechanism of the wounded child within.

It is essential to understand: wounded people, aggressive or closed-off people, are not bad in essence. They are simply beings who have forgotten how to feel safe. Who have lost trust in love. Who live dominated by fear – a fear of being rejected, controlled, humiliated, or misunderstood.

But the true question is not only about others, but about you:

What mask do you wear?

The Illusion of the Ego and the Burden of Attachments

The ego is the fog that prevents you from seeing what already exists within you: boundlessness, stillness, joy, peace. When you identify with the body, you limit yourself to a temporary form. The truth is that you are not your body. You are not your thoughts. You are not the fears or ambitions that drive you.

You are essence. You are spirit. You are eternal presence in the midst of a temporary experience. And when this remembrance returns to you, all the battles of the ego cease.

A Moment of Introspection

I invite you to pause for a few moments.

To breathe deeply.

To let your thoughts settle like dust at the bottom of a vessel of water.

And to ask yourself, with sincerity:

– To what extent do I live from the ego?

– How much of what I think I am is only a mask, a protection, an illusion?

– What lies beyond my roles, my image, my fears and desires?

– Who am I, truly, beyond form, beyond name, beyond past?

The answer must not be rushed. It does not come through analysis, but through presence. Through stillness. Through remembrance.

And when your soul whispers the answer, you will recognize it not because it is logical, but because it will make you feel – at Home.

The Call to Authenticity

This journey toward "home" is not an easy road, but it is without doubt the most valuable. To renounce the masks and the illusions of the ego means to expose yourself, to show your vulnerability. True power lies precisely in this vulnerability, because showing your authentic self is an act of supreme courage. When you stop hiding, you attract into your life people and experiences that resonate with your inner truth.

The process of unmasking illusions is, in fact, a process of liberation. Liberation from the burden of being someone else, liberation from fear and from the need to control. When you begin to live from your essence, from spirit, life gains a flow, an ease. You no longer feel you are struggling against the current, but floating with it, knowing that you are guided by a higher intelligence.

The Soul's Awakening Signals

Sometimes life sends us strong signals to awaken us. A crisis, a loss, an illness, an apparent failure – all of these can, in fact, be messengers. They force us to stop the daily rush and ask essential questions. Who am I, if I am not my profession, my money, or my relationships?

These moments of crisis are disguised gifts, opportunities to transcend old patterns and reconnect with who we truly are.

It is important to listen to our intuition. This gentle yet persistent voice is the voice of your soul. It does not manifest as an agitated thought, but as a calm certainty, a subtle direction. When the mind shouts "be cautious!", intuition may whisper "be brave!". True wisdom is learning to distinguish between the fears of the ego and the callings of the heart.

The Road Home Never Ends

There is no final destination in this journey, because your essence is already "home." The journey is about remembering this truth in every moment. It is a daily practice of presence, of observation, of self-love. Each step, whether small or large, is a return to source, to your divine uniqueness.

And as you awaken, you will realize that your supreme purpose is not to accomplish something grand, but simply to be yourself. And through your simple authentic existence, you give the world the most precious gift.

Conclusion

Life on Earth is like a school of the soul, where every experience becomes a precious lesson. Often, what challenges us most is exactly what helps us grow. A loss, a pain, or a disappointment may seem like heavy burdens, but within them lies a light: a call to authenticity, to the discovery of inner strength.

The true question is not "why is this happening to me?", but "what does my soul want me to learn from this experience?". When we dare to see in this way, reality changes its face. Obstacles transform into steps, fears into opportunities for courage, and sufferings into gateways to compassion.

The journey we walk here is not about perfection, but about remembrance. We were born not to become someone else, but to return to what we already are: beings of light, love, and presence. Every moment in which we choose to be honest with ourselves and let the masks fall is a victory of the soul.

In moments of stillness, when you breathe deeply and let your mind come to rest, you can feel the pulse of eternity within you. It is a space where there is no guilt, no shame, no fear. There is only peace and freedom. And there, in that stillness, you remember that you are infinite and that your purpose here is simple: to bring love into the world, through who you are and through what you do.

Questions for Reflection

– What experiences in my life have helped me discover who I truly am?

– In what ways can I lay aside the mask I wear and live more authentically?

NOTES

Chapter 2

Access to Universal Memories – Remembrance and Past Lives

How I Came to Remember Past Lives

This book is not just a gathering of personal stories, but an opening of the soul.

It represents an invisible thread that unites my experiences across many lives and that, through a mysterious synchronicity, has brought me here and now to share them.

Some of my accounts may seem difficult to understand or even fantastical. That is natural. The human mind has been conditioned to believe only what can be measured and verified. I know that some will read with skepticism, others will judge me, and some may call me a "dreamer." I do not condemn them. Everyone sees through the lens of their own consciousness.

What I set down here are not theories, but realities I have lived. They are living memories, experienced with my whole being, that have transformed me and helped me understand who I am.

I have had moments when I could enter the depths of other people's souls, feeling their unspoken thoughts, hidden pains, or unconfessed joys. This gift is not meant for curiosity or power, but as a great responsibility. The intimacy of a being is sacred and must be respected. That is why I do not give concrete examples and do not mention names. But I can say that each experience has taught me to look at people with more compassion and to understand that beyond masks and words lies a soul seeking light.

The Universe as a Spiral of Memory

I discovered that the universe is not linear, but cyclical. Everything repeats, but never in the same way. It is a subtle spiral, where each turn brings with it an added ray of wisdom. As an old teaching says: *"What has been will be again, and what will be has already been."*

Each life carries echoes of the ones before: unfinished lessons, unended loves, forgotten promises. Nothing is random. Everything is divine orchestration.

For me, the process of remembrance began gradually. Sometimes vivid images appeared, other times intense emotions with no apparent reason. Sometimes it was enough to see a photograph or hear an old song, and within me a door would open to another time. Over time, I understood that what I was experiencing was a touch of the Akashic field – that universal library in which every thought, every action, every moment of existence is preserved.

I also realized something else: the memories shown to me never came randomly. I received only what my soul was ready to understand. It was a process guided by a wisdom greater than my mind.

Perception of Reality and the Limitations of the Mind

Why do some people reject such experiences? Because our perception is filtered by the mind, and the mind is limited by beliefs. It is as if you were looking at the world through a pair of colored glasses: if the lenses are yellow, everything appears yellow; if they are blue, everything appears blue. Reality itself remains what it is, beyond the filters.

Religions, cultures, traditions are also like lenses. Each claims to possess the absolute truth. And yet, if you look with the eyes of the heart, you see that each contains a spark of light, but also the shadows of its own limitation.

I understood that Divine Truth cannot be confined in a dogma, a book, or an institution. It is infinite and alive. It reveals itself directly in the hearts of those who have the courage to search, to question, and to feel beyond the walls of fear.

Perhaps you too, dear reader, have felt that there is more than you were told. Perhaps you have had strange dreams, déjà-vu sensations, or emotions without logical explanation. Perhaps you have met people you felt "close" to from the very first moment. These are not coincidences. They are signs of your soul remembering.

About Akasha – The Space of Universal Memory

The word *"Akasha"* comes from Sanskrit and means *"space"* or *"eternal sky."* In essence, it is the subtle matrix in which the entire memory of existence is preserved. Nothing is lost. Everything that was, is, or will be remains recorded.

My access to this field was not planned. It happened spontaneously, as if an invisible door had opened. At first, I thought it was only my imagination. Then, as the visions became clearer, I understood that it was not a game of the mind, but contact with a space of knowledge that exceeded me.

Why do some have such experiences and others do not? Not because there are "special" souls and "ordinary" ones, but because each has its own rhythm of awakening. Akasha opens only when you are ready to receive what is revealed to you.

Signs of Accidental Access to Akasha

Many people experience Akasha without realizing it. When you step into a place you have never been, but feel a powerful sense of familiarity – that may be a memory. When you repeatedly dream of a scene or an unfamiliar face, it may be the echo of another life.

A déjà-vu can be more than an impression. It can be a window briefly opened, through which your soul shows you that it has been there before.

Some people also receive subtle messages during meditation or even in moments of deep stillness. The information does not come as a clear story, but as states, sensations, fleeting images. Yet they leave behind a certainty: *"I have been there, I have lived this."*

As these experiences repeat, they become clearer and stronger. Not to impress, but to help the soul understand who it is and what it has to learn.

Reflection for the Soul

I invite you to ask yourself a simple question:

What memory, emotion, or dream has returned in your life without a logical reason?

Do not rush to judge it as fantasy. It may be a key. It may be your soul's voice telling you: *"Remember who you are."*

An Inner Guide to Decoding the Messages

As I continued to explore this space of universal memory, I realized that access to it is not enough. It is equally important to understand how to decode the messages you receive.

Akasha does not speak in simple words, but in a language of symbols, emotions, and energies. It is as if you were learning a new language – the language of the soul.

I learned to distinguish between a mere thought that arises and a deep intuition that comes from another plane of consciousness. Intuition does not require logic, but feeling. It is an inner certainty, a "yes" or a "no" that resonates in your heart, even if the mind cannot explain it.

When I received a vision from another life, for example, I did not focus on historical details, but on the lesson my soul needed to learn from that experience. Perhaps it was about forgiveness, about letting go of control, or about choosing love in the face of fear.

The Path to Karmic Healing

Remembrance is not an end in itself, but a tool for healing. Many of our challenges in this life – inexplicable fears, strong attractions or repulsions toward certain people, repetitive behavior patterns – have their roots in past lives.

Akasha offered me the key to understanding these roots. For example, an acute fear of water turned out to be linked to a traumatic experience of drowning in a past life. By becoming aware of the source, I was able to release that emotion and choose a new path.

This process was not always easy. It meant confronting my shadows, reliving sufferings, and forgiving – not only others but also myself. Karmic healing does not mean erasing the past, but integrating it with wisdom. It is as if you were rewriting a chapter of your story, not by deleting the text but by adding a footnote: *"This chapter taught me to be stronger."*

Connection with Others

Another important revelation was the way our lives intersect with those of others. There are no chance encounters. Our souls meet again and again, in different roles, to complete lessons, honor promises, or help each other evolve.

This understanding brought me deep compassion. When someone causes you pain, it is possible that in another life the roles were reversed. Recognizing these karmic connections helps you look beyond personality, at the soul level, and release resentments.

Do not rush to label these ideas. Let them settle in your heart. Perhaps you too will find, in the stillness after a dream or in the moment of a déjà-vu, a piece of your own universal memory. It is time to listen to what it tells you.

What lessons do you think you could learn from your memories?

Conclusion

Remembrance is not a spectacle of the past, but a living bridge to your present. When a memory rises from the field of universal memory, it does not come to hurt you, but to set you free. It brings before you a missing piece of your being's puzzle, so that today you can choose more consciously.

To see the spiral of existence instead of a straight line gives you patience: you understand that everything has a time, a meaning, and a subtle order. You are not here by chance; you came with gifts, with lessons, and with encounters meant to awaken your heart.

Akasha does not reward curiosity, but maturity. It gives you only what you can bear, when you are ready to turn knowledge into wisdom. That is why practice becomes essential: honesty with yourself, daily stillness, discernment between the voice of fear and the whisper of the heart.

When you rest in this presence, the images, symbols, and intuitions begin to weave into a coherent story – your true story.

Karmic healing does not erase what was; it embraces it with gentleness and changes its direction. Forgiveness becomes art, compassion becomes breath, and responsibility becomes freedom. As you honor your memories, you are no longer their prisoner. You are the creator of a new chapter, in which love leads and fear melts into light.

Dare to ask, to feel, and to listen: in this space, your soul shows you the way home.

Questions for Reflection

– What repetitive situation in my life might be my soul's call toward healing and understanding?

– What daily practice (silence, journaling, meditation, prayer) helps me most to distinguish between the mind's fear and the whisper of the heart?

NOTES

Chapter 3

Possible Futures and Destiny

The Akashic field does not contain a single future, but a multitude of possibilities. Every human being constantly has several lines of potential unfolding simultaneously. Usually, there is a main direction – a line of destiny – shaped by the soul's choices, intentions, and karmic lessons. But around this main line, other paths open, subtle branches that can significantly alter the trajectory of a life.

Every decision, every deep thought, every inner transformation can close or open a new version of the future. These versions do not radically depart from the soul's general purpose, but they can change the quality of experience, the pace of learning, or the depth of karmic encounters. It is like a gigantic tree: the trunk is the general destiny, the branches are the choices, and the leaves are the experiences lived. No matter which branch you choose to walk on, you remain within the same tree of your life, but the view and the lessons will be different.

Many people naturally approach the Akashic field before leaving this plane. It is that sacred moment when their whole life flashes before their eyes – like a condensed film, yet full of meaning. This review takes place through the third eye, the spiritual center of inner sight, located in the middle of the forehead. There, in that mysterious space, the soul reconnects with its truth, beyond illusion and fear.

Often, people judge those souls who made predictions about the future that apparently "did not come true." Yet what many do not know is that when someone "sees" a future, they perceive only one among many possibilities. The final reality is continually co-created, influenced by individual choices but also by the collective consciousness – that common field in which our thoughts, fears, and love together shape the path of the world.

The Power of Conscious Choices

The future is neither a punishment nor a reward, but a reflection of what you have chosen to learn. Sometimes the soul chooses the harder path, because within it lies a deeper lesson. Other times, it chooses the gentler path, to integrate joy and gratitude. Both are equally valuable.

Just as a river flows toward the ocean yet can form meanders, waterfalls, or lakes along the way, so your life has a final meaning, but the shape of the journey is molded moment by moment through your decisions. If you choose love, the flow becomes gentler. If you choose fear, obstacles appear and the lessons grow tougher. But the ocean remains the same: the return to the divine source.

Personal Destiny and Collective Destiny

There are moments when individual choices are less visible because you enter a collective destiny. Examples include wars, pandemics, or major social changes. Then the soul is not living only its own lesson, but also the lesson of an entire community, nation, or even humanity. Yet even there, in the midst of a collective storm, each person has the freedom to choose how to respond: with fear or with love, with despair or with wisdom.

The Role of Synchronicities

When you are on your authentic path, life sends you signs. You meet people at the right moment, unexpected opportunities appear, and obstacles turn into lessons. These synchronicities are not coincidences. They are "messages" through which the universal field shows you that you are aligned with your destiny.

But when you feel that everything is blocked, that nothing works, that you stumble at every step, it may be a sign that your soul is asking for a change. Not as punishment, but as an invitation to a new choice.

Healing Through Forgiveness and Joy

These lines are for you, dear soul, as a caress and a calling. Whatever pain you have gone through, however deep the wounds, know this essential truth: healing is possible.

There is no wound that love cannot touch. There is no pain that cannot be transformed through forgiveness. Forgiveness does not mean that the other's actions were right. It does not mean you forget. It means you choose not to carry the burden in your heart anymore. It means you free yourself, not for the other, but for yourself.

Every moment in which you forgive is a moment in which your soul breathes again. And when forgiveness settles within you, joy begins to rise. Joy does not come from a perfect life, but from a heart that has chosen to be grateful even for imperfection.

Turn up the volume of joy in your life. Let your smile be a silent blessing. Let your energy inspire. Because when you heal, you become a lighthouse for others.

Reflection:

Do not ask only "What is my future?", but "What do I choose to create right now?" For the future is not written in stone. It is sculpted in every moment, through your thoughts, emotions, and actions.

The Freedom to Rewrite the Story

True freedom does not mean doing whatever you want, but freeing yourself from old scripts and writing a new story, more aligned with who you truly are. The human mind is often a prison, built on limiting beliefs and accumulated fears. "I am not good enough," "I do not deserve love," "I cannot succeed" — these thought patterns, often inherited or formed after traumatic experiences, create a predetermined future, a destiny of failure or unhappiness.

But, as we have seen, these patterns are not your ultimate reality. They are only a branch your soul chose to explore, with the possibility of leaving it at any time. The moment of "awakening" occurs when you become aware of these patterns. When you observe them without judgment, as old habits of the mind, you can release them. In that space of awareness, the power appears to choose a new thought, a new emotion, a new action. This is, in fact, the magic of co-creation. You are no longer a victim of circumstances but an architect of your reality.

Choosing to forgive yourself for past mistakes, to release resentment, and to embrace joy is an act of sculpting a new future. It is as if you were re-synchronizing your soul's frequency with the vibration of love and abundance.

The Role of the Body in the Creation Process

We must not forget that spirit and physical body are interconnected. The future is not created only through thoughts and intentions, but also through the energy you radiate with your whole body. When you are full of fear or stress, your body tightens, your heart closes, and you emanate a contracting energy. This energy draws contracting experiences into your life.

By contrast, when you are relaxed, full of gratitude and love, your body opens, your heart vibrates, and you emanate an expanding energy. This energy opens doors to new possibilities and attracts people and opportunities aligned with your soul's desires.

Therefore, care for your body through movement, conscious nourishment, and listening to its needs. It is a spiritual act of great importance — a way of honoring the temple in which your Spirit dwells and through which it manifests in this world.

From Intention to Manifestation

The future does not appear from a single intention, but from sustaining a state of being. If you desire a life full of joy, it is not enough to think of joy once. You need to cultivate joy like a plant, every day. You can start with simple gestures: a sincere smile, a walk in nature, a moment of gratitude for small things.

These actions, seemingly mundane, create new neurological and energetic patterns that, over time, build a new reality. Your soul already knows the way. Now your mind must become an ally, not an obstacle. The mind's role is to translate the soul's desires into concrete actions, to plan, to find solutions — not to block the process with its fears and doubts. When the mind and heart work together, an incredible force of manifestation is created.

Guard Your Energy!

On this journey, it is vital to protect your energy. Do not let your joy depend on others, and do not feed on the drama and negativity around you. Choose wisely the people, places, and information with which you surround yourself. You are a radiant being, and your energy is a beacon. Keep it clean and bright so you can navigate the waves of life with confidence.

Remember: every moment is a new starting point. It does not matter what was, but what you choose it to be. What small step can you take today to free yourself from an old burden and make room for joy?

Conclusion

The future is not a verdict, but a living dialogue between your soul and life. The field of possibilities opens before you with every breath, and your choices, states, and intentions give it shape. When you view existence as a spiral instead of a fixed line, both trial and grace gain meaning: you learn, you rise, you refine. And synchronicities become subtle signs that you are nearing the trunk of your authentic destiny.

Choose to cultivate uplifting states — gratitude, gentleness, clarity — and they will attract contexts to match. Forgiveness lightens your steps, and joy illuminates your path. The body, listened to with respect, becomes an anchor for a wakeful consciousness; the mind, quieted, becomes the instrument of the heart. When these dimensions work together, you move from "hoping" to "creating."

You cannot control every branch of the tree of life, but you can choose which one to step on today. You can leave behind old scripts and, moment by moment, write a truer story for yourself. In this act of co-creation, you are never alone: the universal field responds with signs, encounters, ideas. Open yourself, stay curious, stay present. Thus the future becomes not a projected fear, but a living promise of your heart in action.

Questions for Reflection

– What state do I choose to cultivate daily (gratitude, courage, joy, clarity) to align my future with the truth of my heart?

– Which branch of the "tree of life" do I consciously choose to step onto now, and what small action confirms it today?

NOTES

Chapter 4

Memories from Past Lives

Fragments from other times, lived in the silence of the soul.

I remember a life in which I was on Earth... but not the Earth we know today. It was a vast world, covered with forests full of gigantic mushrooms, as tall as trees. The light was gentle, diffuse, and the air vibrated with stillness. I was an adolescent, together with others like me — young, pure beings, running through that world as if we were daydreaming. We needed neither food nor words. At night we slept under deep skies, yet felt neither fatigue nor suffering. Everything was perfect. It was a life without fear or lack, a time of innocence that reminded us what it means to live in harmony with the All.

In another existence, I lived in a world where the duality of good–evil was not enough to describe reality. There, thoughts and actions were not classified only as good or bad, but in at least seven intermediate shades. Every choice went through a subtle process of understanding, and our consciousness was trained to feel the nuances of every intention. It was a world of expanded discernment, where truth was not simplified but honored in all its complexity.

I was not alone. There were more of us — perhaps a few dozen — each with a unique vibration, each carrying within a sphere of knowledge. We were in another dimension, beyond time, where thought becomes reality and matter obeys the will of the heart. There I understood for the first time that there is no "good" or "bad" decision, only experiences that open or close your heart.

In another life, I took on the role of creator. I brought to life beings similar to humans — those later called "Atlanteans." I made a choice: not to tell them who I truly was. I descended among them and lived as one of them. Not out of concealment, but out of love — to understand them, to be close to them. I then discovered that true authority does not come from being worshiped, but from being present and loving unconditionally.

In that existence, the body was not a limitation. I did not feel cold or heat, hunger or thirst — unless I chose to experience them. The body did not age. I did not need sleep. Everything was created by thought — a clear intention was enough to give form to the world around. It was an existence in which matter obeyed consciousness, and consciousness was free from suffering.

All these memories live within me not as stories, but as parallel realities pouring their echoes into the present. I do not write them to impress, but to share. Perhaps you too, dear reader, have had a strange dream, a sensation of déjà vu, an emotion without a logical cause. Perhaps it is not fantasy. Perhaps it is your soul remembering…

Reflection:

If this is not your first life… what has come within you to remember, now?

Atlantis and Its Fall

I remember a life lived in what people would later call Atlantis. It was not only a place, but a sacred space — an island created by intention, in the middle of the ocean, where we, withdrawn from among humans, wished to build a civilization of peace and knowledge.

I arrived there together with those whom we called the Atlanteans — tall, lucid beings, able to shape reality through the power of thought. Each chose a place to live, in harmony with nature and with the subtle laws of creation. Time flowed differently. There was no pain, lack, or suffering. Our society was based on balance, communion, and profound spiritual knowledge.

But, as in all stories of the soul, temptation appeared. After a long time of harmony, in some of the Atlanteans a desire for power awoke. Two camps formed: those who wanted to rule and those who opposed any form of domination. The fracture was not only social, but vibrational. What had been a unified field cracked.

Conflicts grew. In their fury, the Atlanteans began to use the power of the mind not to create, but to control. They manipulated matter, raising waves of earth and hurling them at one another. What had been sacred became unstable. And the island… began to sink.

When I saw the disaster, I flew above the waters, guided not by fear but by an inner calling. The Atlanteans near me, seeing me, remembered that they too could fly. Few were those who reactivated this consciousness. Those who did not find their inner power were swallowed by the waves — not as punishment, but as a lesson for future lives.

With those who survived, I reached a new land. That land would later be known as Egypt. There, we began again. In a more limited form, but with the same desire to keep the ancient wisdom alive. In the place where today the pyramids of Giza rise, we planted the seeds of another civilization — one that, though lost in time, still carries the echo of Atlantis.

Reflection:

What remains of a civilization when it falls? The form disappears, but the memory remains in the soul. What part of you carries such a memory?

Building the Pyramids

After we settled in the realm known today as Egypt, I asked the Atlanteans who had traveled with me if they felt called to build something together. All agreed. I projected into their minds the clear image of a structure — a sacred, universal form: the pyramid.

To keep the origin veiled, we created the stone blocks so that they would appear manually cut, fashioned in the same style as those found in natural quarries. We wished that people of the future would not fully understand how they were made. Only those with an active inner sight could sense the truth.

We raised three pyramids, each aligned precisely with constellations, in a hidden correlation between heaven and earth. The Great Pyramid was clad in light-colored stones, shining under the sun like a beacon of light.

In the heart of the Great Pyramid we created a hidden chamber, where we placed a rhombic crystal. It radiates a white, pure light, remaining suspended in the air — untouched by anything, floating between worlds. To prevent its premature activation, we slightly altered the pyramid's orientation relative to magnetic north.

We also used advanced technologies — what today might be called machines. Yet they had no engines and no fuel. They moved by mental command, extensions of our consciousness. These machines had forks at the front with which they could grasp stones. With these mechanisms we lifted the two smaller pyramids, then we hid the machines in the earth, where they still sleep.

Near the pyramid, I built a dwelling — a two-story house, created through the power of thought. The stones used had the same vibrational essence as the pyramid: purity, balance, clarity. I shaped them and placed them one atop another by thought, leaving in the walls openings in the form of windows and doors — without frames, without panels. It was a house of light.

Upstairs, to the right after the stairs, I created a crystal with triangular faces. Over time, it took the shape of a perfect rhombus — like the cut diamonds of our day. It resembled two pyramids joined at their bases. It was over a meter tall and vibrated at a high frequency.

I arranged a large room and, behind it, a secret chamber. The only entrance was a thick sliding door, integral to the stone wall. In front of this chamber I placed nearly ten tall tables, with slanted tops. If four or five of them were touched in a certain order — starting with the second — the door would open. The code began with the second table.

Inside, I placed several crystals — four or five, each different. Some were colored, and one was white. That white crystal was luminous, emitting an eternal vibration. The energy in that room was so strong that an ordinary person could not withstand it for long. The crystals emitted individual light, each in the color specific to its vibration.

Before leaving, I also shaped the Sphinx — a silent guardian, intentionally left unfinished. By its right ear I placed a stone with a symbolic role. I left a message for those who would come:

When that stone falls without the touch of a being, the pyramid will activate. And the wave of energy released will encompass the entire planet, awakening humanity to a new consciousness.

Parting from the Atlanteans

Before departure, I felt it was time to close a stage. I turned to the Atlanteans and asked, with love and respect, who would wish to remain in the Great

Pyramid to watch over the crystal — that radiant heart which was to remain silent yet alive until humanity was ready to understand it.

One of them volunteered without hesitation. He remained there, not as a guard, but as a conscious being, in a state of deep vigilance, to maintain the balance and protection of the sacred space. I told the others to hide their houses in the earth, by the same power with which they had created them. Thus the dwellings withdrew into the silence of the soil, becoming invisible to the outer eye, yet keeping their vibration untouched.

With a small group of Atlanteans, I then set out for another place on Earth. There, we built a stepped pyramid — a symbol of inner ascension, a reminder to the souls of the future that the path to light is taken step by step. Other similar structures were then created in various corners of the planet and even on other worlds, wherever life allowed consciousness to express itself freely.

Everything was prepared for a final step.

In a common act of renunciation and transcendence, we left our bodies behind — we left them in the water, carried by stillness. Then we flew into the astral, freeing ourselves from the density of matter, to continue the journey beyond forms, beyond time, beyond what the eye can see.

It was not death. It was a return — a step into the great breath of the Universe.

Hidden Truths

The pyramids were not the product of a single age or civilization. They were raised and rebuilt many times, by beings from various civilizations, each leaving part of its mystery in stone. Sometimes we were free builders; other times we were forced to work as giants in the service of others. But the law of balance turned the wheel: those who subjected us became subjects in other lives, and together we continued the cycle of creation.

Beside the Sphinx, I left an engraved message: "We have been here from the beginning." Not for power, but as a reminder of the soul's continuity.

The secrets kept in great libraries, even at the Vatican, are only pale shadows of the truth. True knowledge was not written, but kept in the hearts of those prepared to live it.

Conclusion

Profound truths are not found in books, but in the silence of the heart. The pyramids are not only monuments of the past — they are memories of the spirit, symbols of our journey through ages, through forgetting and remembrance.

Each of us is a thread in the divine weaving of creation. Every life, every form, every lesson lived in pain or joy carries us closer to remembering what we have always been: pure love, unified consciousness.

When we learn to look at one another with the eyes of the soul, without fear, without comparison, without judgment — then the gate to the great mysteries will open again. Not as a privilege, but as a homecoming.

Extending the Conclusion

Everything I have described here is not only a story of the past, but also a calling for the present. The soul's memories do not pour into us to make us cling to them, but to remind us who we are and what power we carry. The pyramids, Atlantis, vanished civilizations — all are mirrors of our own inner journey. They teach us that every fall hides within it the seeds of a rebirth and that nothing is truly lost, only transformed.

Today, humanity stands at a new threshold. Like Atlantis, we live a tension between light and shadow, between love and the desire for control. The choice is ours: we can repeat the mistakes of the past, or we can open the path to a civilization based on consciousness and compassion. The gate is not outside, but within us. When each person remembers their own light, the entire world changes.

The conclusion of these memories is simple and yet profound: the power of spirit is greater than any force of matter. Stone, water, fire, or air obey the awakened consciousness.

Questions for Reflection

– What memory, dream, or inexplicable sensation is your soul telling you is not mere fantasy, but a call to remembrance?

– How can you bring more consciousness and love into your daily life, to honor the lessons of the past and create a brighter future?

NOTES

Chapter 5

Encounters Beyond the Veil

Memories of the Soul

I remember a time when my body was no longer a burden. I no longer needed food, sleep, or air. I was pure consciousness, moving freely through spaces of light, in a dimension where there were no borders or distances. I did not walk or run — I was simply wherever I wished to be.

In that subtle plane, I met other souls. We had no need for words. Communication happened through vibration, through emotion, through the direct flow of thought. What in the material world would take hours of discussion was transmitted there in an instant, like a cascade of understandings.

I met beings I had never known in a human body, yet my soul recognized them at once. It was as if we were finding one another after a long journey, as if we had always been waiting for one another. These meetings were not random — they were parts of me, of my soul family, coming to remind me of what I had been and what I would be.

When I looked at these souls, I saw around them spheres of light, colors that changed with their thoughts. Some shone in serene blue, others radiated gold or emerald green. Each color was a story, a lesson, a unique vibration.

Astral Journeys

On one journey, I reached a place of white light, without beginning or end. Before me was a vast hall, like a library, but without physical books. It was the Akashic Field. There I saw fragments of my lives, but also of others' lives. Everything was connected. Every soul left a trace, a vibration, a song in that immensity.

I then understood that we are never separate. That past, present, and future exist simultaneously and nourish one another.

Meeting Beings of Light

In one of these experiences, I met beings I could call masters. They did not look like humans, but they emanated an overwhelming presence of love and wisdom. They did not speak to me in words, but in vibrations. The message was simple and direct:

"You are what you are seeking. There is no separation. Everything you see is your reflection."

I felt the walls of the ego collapse within me. Every judgment, every fear, every desire to control disappeared. Only a clear truth remained: we are One, and life is merely a game of consciousness discovering itself.

The Lesson of Unconditional Love

Of all my meetings and journeys, the most powerful lesson was unconditional love. Not the love that demands, not the love that fears, but the love that simply is. It does not judge, it does not compare, it does not stop. It pours like an endless fountain.

I understood that when one person hurts another, they do not do it because they are evil, but because they have forgotten who they are. They are a lost soul, caught in fear, in ego, in pain. And the only true response to this forgetting is love.

Love changes not only the other, but especially you. It heals you from within, bringing you back home.

A Reflection for You

Perhaps you too have felt that you were visited in a dream by someone dear who has passed. Perhaps you have sensed that someone watches over you from beyond the veil of the world. It is not an illusion. It is the larger reality that the mind cannot explain, but the soul recognizes at once.

Ask yourself:

– Who visited me in a dream, and what message did they bring?

– What emotions do I feel when I am alone, yet it seems someone is with me?

– Am I willing to believe that love never dies, but transforms?

Conclusion

This chapter is not a plea for life after death, but a reminder: life has no death. Only forms change, but essence remains.

The soul is eternal. Love is eternal. Our meetings are eternal.

What seems an ending is only a new gate. What seems loss is only a reunion prepared for another time.

And so, the true question is not whether we will survive death — but whether we will manage to love enough in life so that, when the veil lifts, we recognize that all we sought was always within us.

The Mission on Earth: To Be a Lighthouse

Beyond all these journeys and remembrances lies an essential question: why did we choose to return to this dimension of density, illusion, and suffering? Why did we choose a body that falls ill, a mind that forgets, and a veil of separation that feels so real? Every soul came here with a mission, a unique calling, and that mission is not about heroic deeds or changing the world on a global scale.

The mission is to be. To remember who you are right here, in the midst of chaos, and to let your light shine.

Your soul came to experience fear and choose love. It came to feel wounds and heal them through forgiveness. It came to remember that you are a creator, not a victim. When you live authentically, aligned with your inner truth, you become — effortlessly — a lighthouse for others.

The Language of Symbols and the Deep Self

The universe speaks to you constantly, but not in simple words. It uses the language of signs, of dreams, of synchronicities. A song you hear on the radio at exactly the right moment, a book that "happens" to fall into your hands, an animal crossing your path — these are, in fact, coded messages.

They are subtle clues that you are on the right path or that you need to recalibrate your direction. To be aware of these signs is to live in a continual dialogue with the Universal Spirit, with that Infinite Intelligence that orchestrates everything.

The Role of Wounds and Suffering

There is no perfect spiritual path free of pain. On the contrary, suffering is often our best teacher. It is the catalyst that forces us to look within, to face our fears, and to free ourselves from illusions.

Many of the wounds we carry were created by ourselves in other lives, through unconscious choices. But now, in this life, we have the chance to look at them, accept them, and heal them.

To heal a soul's wound does not mean to erase it, but to transform it into a source of wisdom and compassion. From the darkest place, the purest light can arise.

Remembrance and the Practice of Presence

Remembering past lives and meetings beyond the veil is not a caprice, but a natural process. Yet more important than remembering the past is living fully in the present.

The present is the only moment in which you can choose, love, create. To anchor yourself in the now is to connect with your essence.

When you are present, the mind quiets, and the soul's subtle voice becomes easier to hear. This is, in essence, the simplest and most profound form of spirituality.

Each breath is a return to source, a chance to reconnect with the truth that you are a particle of divinity.

An Invitation to a New Beginning

It does not matter what happened yesterday or in past lives. What matters is what you choose to do now.

Choose to forgive yourself. Choose to love, without fear. Choose to be yourself.

Your path is unique, and your destiny is a masterpiece you create with every conscious choice.

Extended Conclusion

Encounters beyond the veil show us that reality is far vaster than what we perceive through the physical senses. They remind us that life does not begin at birth and does not end at death, but is an endless thread passing through countless forms and experiences.

The true power of these memories does not lie in their spectacle, but in the simple lesson they bring: love and presence are the key. When we learn to be present and to love unconditionally, we align with the flow of the universe.

The soul does not seek titles, victories, or glory. It seeks to experience, to grow, and to return again and again to its source. That is why every meeting, every suffering, every joy are steps on the same ladder of remembrance.

Unconditional love is the highest truth. You do not need to wait for death to feel it. You can live it here and now, in the way you look, in the way you touch, in the words you speak, and in the silences you keep.

If you choose to live in this way, you will no longer fear the end. You will know that every moment is, in fact, a gate to eternity.

Questions for Reflection

– How would my life change if I saw every person I meet as an eternal soul, not just a passing body?

– What signs or synchronicities are showing me, right now, that I am accompanied and guided from beyond the veil?

NOTES

Chapter 6

Memories of Power and the Lesson of Love

Power Seen from Within

I was there where power was portioned out in whispers, far from the eyes of the crowds. In "dark" halls, around large tables, a few people decided the destinies of millions. They were not simple political or administrative decisions. They were strategy games in which countries were divided like pieces on a cosmic chessboard. Whoever had more commanded. Whoever had less was sacrificed without remorse.

In those times, a person's value was not given by their soul, but by the influence they could wield. There I understood how fragile the world's balance is and how easily the masses allow themselves to be led by pride, fear, and promises.

But life is a perfect circle. The one who raises the sword will sooner or later feel its edge. The one who ignores others' suffering will become, in another life, the very one who suffers. And only then is the lesson of power truly understood.

The Law of Balance

Have you been given the bread and the knife? Then you have also been given the responsibility to use them with love. If you choose to share, the light returns to you. If you choose to keep only for yourself, the shadow will follow your steps.

I saw leaders living in luxury, surrounded by riches and flattery, passing indifferently by people with pensions so small they could barely buy medicine or daily food. And I knew then that those leaders would become, in another life, those very forgotten people. Not as punishment, but as experience.

Indifference is a subtle form of cruelty. Sometimes doing nothing hurts more than a direct blow. When you have the power to change something and choose to remain silent, you create a wound not only in others, but also in yourself.

The Lesson of Suffering

There is no being that escapes this law. Each of us reaps what we sow. And if we refuse to learn through love, we will learn through suffering. I have lived this. I have been both the one who carelessly decided others' fate and the one who shivered with cold, unable to pay for a loaf of bread. I felt both extremes, and only then did I understand that power, devoid of love, inevitably turns into pain.

Suffering is not a curse, but a teacher. It leads you step by step to a greater question: What have I done, thought, or chosen to arrive here? And the answer, however painful, becomes liberating.

A Vision from the Astral

In an astral journey, I reached a vast hall, bathed in light. Before me stood a rectangular stone table. Around it, three wise men looked on with seriousness, yet with love. On that table I saw people's spirits like living flames. Each soul radiated exactly what it carried within: love or fear, light or shadow, compassion or pride.

Everything was perfectly balanced. No deed remained without an echo. If you gave an order for others to do evil in your stead, the responsibility remained yours. Offices, titles, hierarchies did not matter. The flame of the soul showed exactly who you are.

I understood then that no one can deceive this law. You can lie to people, hide the truth from the world's eyes, but you cannot hide your real vibration. It is visible beyond the veil, where everything is clear and simple.

The Lesson of Love

Through all these experiences, a single truth rose above all: power without love destroys, but power with love transforms.

If you hold a leadership role, it is not to dominate but to serve. If influence has been given to you, it is not to hoard, but to share. True greatness is not measured by how many bow before you, but by how many rise through you.

Love is the only force that is not consumed when you give it. The more you give, the more you grow. It is the only "wealth" you take with you beyond death.

A Reflection for the Soul

Have you ever asked yourself what you do with the power you have, however small it may be? You do not need to be a member of parliament or a ruler. Each of us has influence — in the family, at work, in the community.

Ask yourself:

– Do I choose indifference, or do I choose to be support?

– Do I choose to wound, or to lift up?

– Do I choose to keep only for myself, or to share with others?

Conclusion

My memories of power are not told to judge, but to remind. Power is a gift, but also a test. If you use it selfishly, it will turn against you. If you use it with love, it will lift you and those around you.

The universe never errs. Everything returns; everything balances. What now seems an unfair advantage becomes tomorrow a painful lesson. What now seems suffering becomes tomorrow a hidden blessing.

And in the end, the only thing that truly remains is not title, office, or wealth — but the love you have given.

The Rise and Fall of the Illusion of Control

Memories of power reveal a fundamental illusion: that of absolute control. Those who hold power often believe they can shape reality at will, ignoring the universal laws of cause and effect.

True power does not come from having control over others, but from controlling yourself — mastering your ego, managing your emotions, and aligning your actions with your heart. This inner power is the only one that remains, even when outer circumstances change.

The Lesson of Collective Responsibility

The visions from halls of power emphasize not only individual responsibility but also collective responsibility. Society is a mirror of each of our consciousness. You cannot have loveless leaders in a society full of love.

When you choose to be indifferent to an injustice, even a small one, you allow that energy to grow. Likewise, when you choose to love, to forgive, and to place yourself in service to others, you contribute to a collective field of love. This is real power: changing the world through your own inner transformation.

From the Karmic Cycle to the Cycle of Consciousness

The law of balance is not a condemnation, but an invitation to awakening. The soul is not placed in difficult situations to be punished, but to have the chance to choose consciously — this time — another path.

Thus the karmic cycle of action and reaction becomes a cycle of consciousness, of evolution and understanding.

An Invitation to a New Way of Being

Do not ask how to possess power, but how to use it. Do not wish to be respected; wish to be a model of love. Do not seek validation outside yourself, but in the balance and peace you feel within.

This is the true triumph of the spirit.

Extended Conclusion

Power is a sacred fire. It can light the way for many, or burn everything around — it depends on how you choose to use it. The lessons of the past, whether personal or collective, show clearly that every act of indifference, egoism, or cruelty returns to the one who sowed it. But likewise, every gesture of love, however small, brings light that multiplies endlessly.

The soul comes to Earth not to conquer, but to learn. Outer power is only a passing stage; inner power, born of love and wisdom, remains with you beyond lifetimes.

Each of us holds a form of power — over our words, our thoughts, our actions. And each choice becomes a seed that will blossom one day. That is why it is worth asking ourselves always: what am I planting today in the garden of my soul and of the world?

True greatness does not mean being above others, but lifting others beside you. In this way, power becomes love, and love becomes eternity.

Questions for Reflection

– How am I currently using my inner power — to control or to heal?

– What do I choose to pass on: fear and indifference, or love and compassion?

NOTES

Chapter 7

Cyclical Lives – Circles of Existence

The Circle of Life

Life is not a straight line with a definitive beginning and end. Life is a circle that repeats itself over and over, in other forms, in other bodies, in other circumstances. Just as spring returns after every winter, so the soul is reborn after every death.

We do not live only a single existence, but hundreds, perhaps thousands. Each life is a new chance to learn the lessons we postponed, to heal the wounds we left open, to fulfill the promises we made. Nothing is lost; everything is preserved in the invisible fabric of spirit.

What seems like chance is often only the echo of a past action. Perhaps you met someone and immediately felt closeness or rejection without knowing why. Perhaps you lived a situation that felt familiar, like a déjà vu. These are not coincidences. They are the soul's memories rising to the surface.

The Law of Return

In the universe nothing remains unpaid. Everything we do, say, or think is a seed. And every seed bears fruit, sooner or later. If you sow love, you will reap love. If you sow hatred, you will reap hatred. If you lift someone up, you too will be lifted. If you wound, you will feel the pain on your own skin.

This law is not a punishment. It is a universal balance, a perfect mechanism of existence. The universe does not punish or reward in the human sense. It simply balances. Everything you emit returns to you so that you may understand.

You can run from people, you can hide your deeds, but you cannot run from your own vibration. It accompanies you everywhere, in this life and in those to come.

Lessons of Compassion

Why do we need so many lives? Because the soul needs to learn compassion. And compassion is not learned from theory, but from direct experience.

In one life you are rich, in another poor. In one you command, in another you obey. In one you are the one who loves, in another you are the one who rejects. Thus the soul lives all roles until it understands that there is no real separation between "me" and "the other."

Compassion means to feel another's pain as if it were your own. And to arrive there, you must have been both executioner and victim, master and servant. Gradually, the soul becomes gentler, wiser, more attentive.

The Illusion of Power

Many are deceived by power. They believe that wealth, position, or prestige makes them invincible. They allow themselves to abuse, to humiliate, to think they are superior. But outer power is only a temporary loan.

Today you are up, tomorrow down. Today you are the one who decides, tomorrow you will be the one who submits. The wheel of life turns constantly. No one escapes. And when you feel on your own skin exactly what you caused others, you will understand that true power is not found in control, but in love.

Everything built on domination collapses. Everything built on love remains.

The Shadow of the Ego

The ego is the greatest obstacle on the path to awakening. It always whispers: "You are better. You deserve more. You must be first." But the truth is different: what you do to another, you do to yourself.

The ego creates the illusion of separation. And when we live in this illusion, we cling to comparisons, competitions, judgments. Yet every mask we wear will melt, sooner or later, before the law of return.

Then we will understand that there are no "others." There are only mirrors of our own consciousness.

Mysteries Beyond Us

People seek mysteries in stars, in planets, in vanished civilizations. But the greatest mystery is your own soul. Who were you 500 years ago? What role did you play 1,000 years ago? Where will you be in other lives to come?

If you do not know these things, then you do not know where you come from nor where you are going.

True knowledge begins with the question: Who am I, beyond this body and this time?

The Call to Awakening

Today humanity is called to remember more quickly. We no longer need hundreds of lives to understand simple lessons. We now have the chance to learn through awareness, through reflection, through love.

What once was learned through repeated suffering can now be understood through a single choice: the choice not to wound any longer. The choice to see in others the face of your own being. The choice to love.

Final Reflection

Ask yourself:

– What lessons does life repeat for me again and again?

– In what situations do I find myself over and over, in different forms?

– What if I were to learn now, through awareness, what once I had to learn through pain?

Cyclical lives are not a condemnation, but a chance. The chance to rise, to become better, to draw nearer to the essential truth: we are One.

And when you feel this in your heart, you will know that you are not trapped in a circle of pain, but in a spiral of evolution.

The Spiral of Evolution: Beyond Illusion

Unlike the circle, the spiral does not close in on itself — it rises. Each rotation is a step forward, an ascent toward a higher consciousness. However often we return to the same lessons, each time we do so from a different position, wiser than before. You are no longer the same person who erred yesterday. You are an evolved version, able to see beyond illusion.

Illusion is what keeps us bound by the chains of time and form. It makes us believe we are only a passing body, a personality with a name and a past. It convinces us that we need external validation, possessions, power. But these are only stage props in a play. The true spectator — your soul — knows the play will end and you will leave the stage.

True liberation comes from recognizing the essential truth: your essence is eternal and inseparable from the whole universe. You are not a stray fragment, but a divine spark, a piece of infinity. With each life, you remember this truth a little more. Every suffering, every joy, every failure or triumph is only a clue guiding you back home.

The Alchemy of Suffering and Joy

If life is a circle, then suffering and joy are its two hemispheres. One cannot exist without the other. Just as you cannot understand light without knowing darkness, you cannot know deep joy without having been touched by pain.

Suffering is a harsh yet effective master. It cracks the shell of the ego, forces us to look within and face our shadows. When everything you built collapses, when you feel alone, abandoned, or wounded, you are forced to seek a support that does not depend on the outer world. This search leads you to your inner source of strength, to your eternal essence.

Joy, on the other hand, is a subtle reward. It does not spring from material acquisitions or others' applause. True joy appears when you are aligned with your authentic self. It is the feeling of peace that embraces you after you have forgiven, of fulfillment after you have helped someone, of connection after you have loved unconditionally. These moments of joy are signs that you are on the right path, on the ascending spiral of evolution.

The Power of Forgiveness and Acceptance

Forgiveness is an essential lesson we learn in this endless cycle. It is not only about forgiving others, but especially about forgiving yourself. When you forgive your past mistakes — those of this life and of previous ones — you release blocked energy and allow yourself to advance. Every wound you carry from the past is an anchor binding you to a cycle you need to complete.

Acceptance is forgiveness's twin sister. Accept that you cannot change what has been. Accept that each person and each event appeared on your path for a purpose. Not to punish you, but to teach you. Once you accept this reality, the burden lifts, and the road opens before you.

Perfecting the Spiral

When you reach the point where you can love others as yourself, when you understand that they are mirrors of your own soul, the spiral nears perfection. Then you no longer need the cycle of births and deaths to learn your lessons. You have reached a state of pure consciousness, of unity with the whole. You are freed from illusion.

This is not an end, but a transformation. You become a guide, a lighthouse for those still in the labyrinth of existence. You use the wisdom you have gathered to light the way for others. Then you no longer live to learn, but to serve. You are no longer a prisoner of the circle, but a conscious part of the spiral that continues to rise, carrying within it the unconditional light of love.

Extended Conclusion

Cyclical lives are not a punishment, but a privilege through which the soul widens its heart until it embraces everything. The circle of existence brings us back to the same themes, each time with greater clarity, until we consciously choose love instead of fear. The law of return does not "punish," it gently educates: it brings before us exactly what we need to become more whole. Where we judged, life invites us to understand; where we wounded, life calls us to heal; where we were indifferent, life awakens compassion.

The spiral of evolution lifts the circle from the repetitive plane into the vertical plane of consciousness. It does not ask for perfection, but for sincerity — the courage to admit when we are wrong and the gentleness to begin again. Forgiveness becomes the bridge by which the soul crosses from past to present, and acceptance the root of a peace no longer dependent on circumstances. In this inner place, power no longer means control, but the capacity to give light without exhausting yourself.

To remember who you are is to see in every person a part of yourself and in every happening a portion of your lesson. Thus, the circle no longer constricts, but embraces; it no longer closes you in, but expands you. And when love becomes your natural choice, you discover that all your lives have pursued the same aim: the conscious return to the One.

Questions for Reflection

— What "repeating lesson" keeps appearing to me in different forms, and how can I now choose a loving response instead of an old reflex?

— What concrete act of forgiveness (toward myself or another) can free me today and lift me one step on the spiral of evolution?

NOTES

Chapter 8

Prisoner or Free on Planet Earth

Beyond Repetition

Few people manage to see beyond the repetitive cycles of life on Earth. Most live day by day, convinced that "now" is all that exists. And yet, reality is far vaster, deeper, more mysterious than what we perceive with our eyes.

What we live today is only a new loop of an ancient cycle. Our manifestations — of spirits and of all living beings — are rooted in forgotten pasts. Nothing appears by chance. Everything repeats, in different forms, yet with the same message: you came to learn.

The Illusion of the Present

Many say, "I live in the present." But the present is not a blank page. It is the result of a much older preparation, of decisions made in other lives, in other times. If in front of you there is an obstacle, a friend, or an enemy, know that all of these are the seeds you yourself once planted.

The present is your inheritance. And the way you choose to live it writes your future.

The Lessons of Repetition

On Earth, everything repeats. The beginning becomes the end, and the end is reborn again as a beginning. Civilizations have flourished and perished countless times. Humanity has gone through the same temptations, the same mistakes, the same struggles for supremacy.

If today you believe you have discovered something "new," remember: what you discover is only a renewed form of a truth lived a thousand times. True novelty is not the invention, but the consciousness with which you repeat the experience.

Changing Roles

In this endless repetition, the only thing that changes is the role you play. Today you are the one who dominates and wounds; in another life you will be the one wounded. Today you are the one who offers love; in another life you will receive the same love you have given.

Only through direct living — by feeling on your own skin the consequence of your deeds — do you come to truly understand. No book and no master can replace experience.

That is why every deed matters. Every word you leave in the world will return. Every thought you cultivate creates your future.

Your Choice

If you let your being be led by pride and arrogance, you prepare suffering for yourself. If you choose compassion and wisdom, you create peace and light.

Seek to see beyond time. And even if you do not always succeed, choose to do the good that stands within your reach. In those small gestures, seemingly insignificant, lies the power to break the cycles of pain.

Less-Evolved Souls

Those who do harm are not "punished" by someone outside. They simply have not yet understood the law of repetition. They are young souls, still playing dangerously with the energy of life. They cannot see beyond the illusion of time, and therefore do not realize they will be forced to relive all that they have sown.

Thus my warning is simple: beware of harm and judgment. Do not respond in kind. Choose to know the truth and to live it.

From Prisoner to Creator

Our purpose on Earth is not to control or dominate. Our purpose is to become creators. But how can you be an authentic creator if you let your life be led by pride, by fear, by the desire to be "right"?

Your real value is not found in how many people are beneath you, but in how much you have raised yourself.

A prisoner is one who repeats the same lessons without understanding. Free is the one who consciously chooses to create good.

Examine Yourself

Examine your being. Look into your consciousness. Ask yourself: Why am I living this again? What lesson am I being asked to learn? If you waste your life chasing only what others do, you will be forced to return again and again.

But if you choose to look honestly at your mistakes and learn from them, you have already taken a step toward freedom.

Beyond Motives

Behind every action there is a motive. If the motive is pure and good, then you have opened a gate toward evolution. If your motive is selfish, you will remain trapped in the circle.

You have a choice: remain a prisoner of repetition or become free through understanding.

Final Reflection

Ask yourself:

– Am I living now for the ego or for the soul?

– What are the things that repeat in my life?

– If I were to see the world as my mirror, what would I see?

The truth beyond the human is not a mystery hidden in libraries, but a simple truth: everything repeats until you choose love.

And when you choose love, you are no longer a prisoner of time, but a creator of eternity.

The Journey to True Freedom

To be free on planet Earth does not mean detaching from everything around you. True freedom is not an escape, but a state of being reached through deep understanding. You are truly free when you no longer need to repeat the same painful lessons, because you have chosen to learn them through awareness.

Humanity stands at a crossroads. We have a unique chance to shorten the path, to spare future generations needless suffering. The tools are at our disposal: ancestral knowledge, intuition, and above all the power of love. When you choose to act from love, you are no longer a puppet of karma, but a conscious creator. By breaking the cycle, you offer yourself — and the entire universe — a priceless gift: the possibility to advance.

Signs of Liberation

How do you know you are on the right path — on the spiral of evolution and not stuck in the circle of repetition? The signs are subtle yet clear.

First, you notice that negative situations no longer repeat: you do not attract the same kind of toxic partner, the same conflicts at work, the same suffering. The lesson has been integrated, and life brings new challenges at a higher, more conscious level.

Then, you feel an inner peace that does not depend on outcomes. Fear quiets, anxiety transforms into calm, and your trust in the meaning of your experiences deepens.

In addition, compassion expands: you no longer judge, because you understand that each person carries their own karmic lessons. The desire to help arises from connection, not from superiority.

Earth, a School of Wisdom

Planet Earth is a school of souls, a cosmic laboratory where consciousness refines itself. We did not come here to rule over one another, but to learn together. From conflicts to innovations, from love to war — all are collective lessons.

Your role is crucial. With every act of kindness, every thought of love, every conscious choice, you contribute to the rise of collective consciousness. You are not alone; you are an essential part of an evolving whole.

Conclusion: Becoming the Master of Destiny

You are not a victim of circumstances, but the architect of your own reality. You are not the prisoner of fate, but a creator of your destiny. Recognize your power — not to dominate, but to serve; not to accumulate, but to share; not to judge, but to understand.

When you rise above the illusion of time and matter, you discover that the truth beyond the human is a lived state. All your cycles and repetitions become a road to freedom: the freedom to love unconditionally, to forgive yourself, and to be, simply, light.

What step will you take today to free yourself from a cycle of the past?

Extended Conclusion

True freedom begins the moment you assume that you are the author of your vibration. You cannot control all circumstances, but you can choose the cause you set in motion now: the intention, the thought, the motivation behind each gesture. There the chain of repetition breaks. When you consciously choose to respond from the heart rather than react from the ego, you rewrite not only your story, but also a small part of the world's story.

Repetition does not disappear through denial, but through understanding. Observe your patterns gently, not with guilt. Ask them what they came to teach you. Sometimes they ask for boundaries, other times for forgiveness, other times for the courage to say "yes" to life. As you respond consciously, the circle becomes a spiral: you return to familiar places, but with more light.

To be a creator means to align motivation, emotion, and action. A pure motive without action remains a dream; action without heart becomes empty effort. When all three meet, reality responds with synchronicities: doors open, the right people appear, and old knots untie without struggle.

Do not measure progress by applause or immediate results, but by the peace that remains in you after you have chosen love. There freedom is born: not in perfect control of life, but in the deep trust that whatever comes is a bridge to more consciousness. Thus, from prisoner of repetition you become a pilgrim of eternity — and each step, however small, is an act of light.

Questions for Reflection

– What pattern (situation, relationship, emotion) keeps repeating in my life, and what new intention can I plant today to transform it?

– What small, concrete gesture can I make in the next 24 hours to choose love instead of the ego's automatic reaction?

NOTES

Chapter 9

Methods for Healing the Soul

Why Does the Soul Need Healing?

When you say "healing," people usually think of the body — of visible wounds, illnesses, palpable pains. Yet the deepest wounds are not on the skin, but in the soul. They are unseen, but felt in every thought, in every emotion, in every choice.

An unhealed soul lives in fear, in guilt, in shame, or in hatred. A wounded soul passes on wounds, because what we do not heal in ourselves, we give to those around us. Thus the chains of pain are born.

But the good news is this: any wound can be healed — no matter how deep, how old, how heavy.

The First Signs of Soul Wounds

You may not know your soul is wounded. You may believe that "this is just life": full of suffering, hardships, and lack. But the signs of inner wounds are clear:

- you feel you are never good enough, no matter what you do;
- you cannot fully rejoice, even when you have reasons;
- you repeat the same mistakes, the same relationships, the same sufferings;
- you feel empty inside, even if you have outer success;
- you find it hard to forgive, to love, or to receive others' love.

All of these show that your soul is asking for healing.

Forgiveness — The Key to Liberation

There is no healing without forgiveness. Forgiveness is the soul's medicine. It does not change the past, but it changes the way the past lives within you.

To forgive does not mean accepting evil as good. It does not mean forgetting or minimizing the pain. It means you choose not to carry the wound within you anymore — that you let it go.

You may say, "I can't forgive; it's too much." And it is natural to feel that. But forgiveness is not done all at once — it is done step by step. Each choice to release resentment, each breath in which you say "I let you go," is an act of healing.

Healing Through Love

If hatred and fear sicken, love heals. Not romantic, conditional love, laden with expectations, but simple, pure love — the one that says: "I give you permission to be yourself. And I give myself permission to be me."

This love always begins within you. You cannot truly love another if you do not learn to love yourself — not selfishly, not with pride, but with gratitude for being an expression of the divine.

When you begin to look at yourself with gentleness, your soul breathes again. And from that moment, love becomes the medicine for every wound.

Healing Through Truth

Another essential step is to acknowledge the truth. You cannot heal a wound if you deny it. You cannot heal a trauma if you say, "It doesn't matter; it's over."

Healing requires the courage to face what hurts — not to remain in pain, but to release it.

Ask yourself with sincerity: What am I hiding within? What do I avoid feeling? What am I afraid to acknowledge?

Often the wound does not disappear because we have raised walls around it. But walls do not heal; they only hide. And what you hide continues to wound you in silence.

Truth, however painful, is the first step toward freedom.

Healing Through Acceptance

After truth comes acceptance. Acceptance is not resignation, not "it was meant to be." Acceptance is acknowledging that what was, was. You cannot change the past, but you can change how you allow it to influence your present.

Acceptance brings peace. Peace is the soil in which love can bloom. And from this love, the soul is reborn.

Healing Through Gratitude

It may seem hard to grasp, but gratitude is one of the most powerful forms of healing. When you learn to say "thank you" even for your pains, your soul rises to another level of consciousness.

Not because pain is good, but because it was your teacher — because it taught you what otherwise you would not have learned.

Gratitude transforms the wound into wisdom.

Healing Through Joy

Healing is not only about crying, releasing, and confronting shadows. It is also about bringing in joy — simple, authentic joy: looking at the sky, smiling, embracing, creating something beautiful.

The soul does not heal only through analysis, but through living. Let your soul rejoice. Do not postpone happiness until "everything is perfect." Perfection never comes. Joy is here and now.

Healing Through Spirituality

Ultimately, healing of the soul is not complete without a conscious connection to the Divine. It does not matter what you call it: God, Source, Universe, Light. What matters is recognizing that you are not alone.

There is a Force greater than you — a Force that sustains you, loves you, and calls you home. When you open your soul to this Force, all wounds begin to soothe.

Prayer, meditation, silence — these are paths by which the soul reconnects to its source. And there, in that connection, healing is complete.

Final Reflection

Healing the soul is a journey. It is not done in a day, nor in a week. But every step counts. Every choice to forgive, to love, to tell the truth, to accept, to be grateful, to live joy, to connect with the Divine — all are stones on the road toward inner freedom.

Ask yourself:

— What wound do I still carry within me?

— What could I forgive today?

— What do I choose to let go of?

Healing is not a luxury. It is the destiny of every soul. And you, dear reader, are called to live it. For when your soul heals, the whole world heals through you.

The Journey of the Heart: From Prisoner to Guide

After the soul begins to heal, the journey does not end. In fact, it truly begins. This healing is not a final goal, but a transformation — a passage from being a prisoner of the past to being the guide of your own destiny and of others. When you leave your wounds behind, you do not forget them; you transform them into wisdom and compassion.

A healed soul becomes a source of light. It no longer seeks outer validation, having found it within. It is no longer led by fear, but by love. And from this deep love, it releases a wave of energy that can touch and heal other souls. Then you no longer live to receive, but to give.

To Be a Point of Source

Imagine that every soul is a river. If the spring is blocked by resentments, unforgiven pains, and traumas, the water cannot flow freely — it stagnates and grows turbid. Healing is the process of releasing these blockages, of clearing the spring. Once the spring is pure, the river can flow freely. And its pure water can nourish the earth, give life to plants, and quench the thirst of other beings.

You are such a river. You have a unique chance to become a point of source — a channel through which love and healing flow into the world. You do not need to be a spiritual master or a guru. You only need to be a human who chose to heal. Your actions, your words, even your presence become a manifestation of this healing. When you are healed, you do not need to do anything special to help others. Your inner light will light their way.

The True Meaning of Service

A healed soul understands the true meaning of service. Service is not an obligation, but a joy — a natural response to being full of love. You no longer help out of guilt or the desire to be appreciated, but from the pure desire to contribute to the common good.

True service needs no audience. It can be a smile offered to a stranger, a hand extended to a friend, a kind word spoken. These simple acts, born from a space of healing, have an incredible power to transform. They are seeds you plant in a world that needs hope.

A Future of Consciousness

Healing of the individual soul is the first step toward collective healing. As more and more people choose to face their wounds, the global consciousness rises. Chains of pain break, and bridges of love and understanding are built.

This is humanity's destiny: to free itself from the past and create a future based on compassion. Every step you take to heal yourself is a step you take for all of us. For in the end, we are not separate souls, but an interwoven network of light.

The end of this journey is not a point, but an expansion — an expansion of consciousness, of love, and of freedom. A state in which you are no longer defined by your wounds, but by the light you offer the world.

Extended Conclusion

Healing the soul is a delicate art between truth, gentleness, and perseverance. It rushes nothing, yet it does not postpone courage. It begins by placing the light of consciousness upon the place that hurts and continues through simple steps, faithfully repeated: conscious breathing, forgiveness spoken in a low voice, small gestures of kindness toward yourself and others. Over time, the wound ceases to dictate your identity and becomes a chapter that has ennobled you.

A useful practice is the "healing triad": (1) name what you feel ("right now I feel fear/shame/anger"); (2) embrace the sensation without judging it ("it is human; I can sit with it safely"); (3) choose one small action aligned with love (a message of forgiveness, a pause, a prayer). Repeated, the triad rewires the pathways of heart and mind, and the blocked energy begins to flow.

Daily gratitude — three true things for which you say "thank you" — lifts the vibration of the entire day, and a few minutes of conscious silence in the morning re-anchors the soul in Source. Do not forget the body: gentle movement, enough water, and settled sleep are part of spiritual healing. The body is the temple in which grace works.

When love becomes your baseline response, it does not mean you no longer feel pain; it means you no longer allow pain to steer your direction. Then you understand: you are not your wound — you are the vast space in which the wound has healed. And from that space, your presence becomes medicine for the world.

Questions for Reflection

– What truth do I avoid looking at directly, and what is the first gentle step by which I can honor it today?

– What concrete act of forgiveness (toward myself or another) can I take in the next 24 hours?

Notes

Chapter 10

Healing the Soul

The human soul is like a crystal vessel: transparent, fragile, yet able to reflect light in a thousand colors. Throughout life, each of us passes through trials, losses, and unseen wounds that leave deep traces within. These scars are not visible to the eye, but they are felt in the heart's silence, in sleepless nights, in unspoken longings.

Sometimes the pain overwhelms us so much that we come to believe our soul has shattered beyond repair. But the truth is that, like a broken mirror that still reflects light, the wounded soul carries within it the power to rise, to find itself, to be reborn.

Healing the soul does not mean forgetting. It does not mean erasing memories or denying the past. Healing means looking at the wound with gentleness, washing it with tears, and allowing the light of love to seep into its cracks. It is an inner journey — often long and painful — but one that leads toward stillness, freedom, and meaning.

The Origin of Our Wounds

Soul wounds do not appear all at once. They gather over time, like raindrops slowly carving stone, leaving marks hard to erase. Sometimes we do not even realize when they began, but we feel their weight in the heart and wonder why our steps suddenly grow heavy.

The loss of a loved one is among the deepest sources of pain. Death, illness, or separation leaves an immense emptiness, and the soul, not knowing how to fill the void, remains wounded. Longing becomes a silent wound, opened again each time we remember the smile or voice of the one who left.

Other wounds are born when our trust is betrayed. Friends who abandoned us, loves that turned into harsh words, promises not kept — all leave invisible yet painful scars. Rejection makes us doubt our worth and sometimes believe we are not deserving of love.

Often the oldest wounds come from childhood. A harsh word, lack of affection, a sense of insecurity, or even emotional abuse dig deep fissures. Hidden away, they continue to influence our choices and relationships even in adulthood.

Not all wounds come from relationships. Sometimes the wound springs from lack of meaning — from a life lived in haste, unanchored, without a clear purpose. A person may feel that no matter what is achieved on the outside, something is missing inside. This inner emptiness can hurt as much as the loss of a dear person.

First Steps Toward Healing

To begin healing, the first step is acknowledgment. Just as a doctor cannot treat an unseen illness, the soul cannot heal from a pain we deny. Many people carry inner burdens for years, hiding them beneath smiles or outer success. But unhealed pain does not disappear; it smolders.

Denial is like an untreated physical wound: it may appear closed on the surface, but within it continues to fester. True courage begins when we stop, look within, and admit: Yes, I am hurting. Yes, I carry wounds. Yes, I need healing.

The second step is acceptance. Acceptance is not resignation. It means to look gently at the present reality, to stop fighting against our own pain, and to open the door to light. From that moment, healing becomes possible.

The Power of Forgiveness and Compassion

Among all keys to healing, forgiveness is the hardest — and the most liberating. The wounded soul carries not only scars, but chains: the chains of resentment, anger, and bitterness. Sometimes these weigh heavier than the wound itself.

Forgiveness is not about the other; it is about us. It does not say "what happened was right," it says: "I choose not to let the wound run my life anymore." In the moment we forgive, we release the soul's energy and allow it to breathe again.

If forgiveness breaks the chains, compassion is the balm that heals. Compassion shows us that the one who hurt us is also a wounded soul. And above all, compassion expands toward ourselves: we stop judging so harshly and choose to say, "I have erred, but I deserve forgiveness. I have fallen, but I can rise."

Faith and Inner Light

There are wounds that only faith can touch. Faith is like an unseen hand supporting us when we feel we can no longer go on. It does not erase suffering overnight, but it reminds us that we are not alone.

In prayer, tears do not fall into emptiness. They become a bridge between us and the divine source of love. In meditation, thoughts quiet and space opens for inner peace. In nature, the soul remembers it belongs to a greater whole.

Faith — whatever its form — is like a candle lit in a dark room. The darkness may be dense, but a single ray of light changes everything.

Healing Through Simple Gestures

The soul's healing is not lived only through great revelations, but also through small, daily acts. Writing, art, music, and dance are doors through which pain transforms into beauty. A walk in the forest or a few minutes of conscious breathing can bring the same calm as a prayer.

Every ritual of presence is a step toward reconstruction. Even the simple gesture of saying "today I choose peace" has the power to set the soul upon a new path.

From Pain to Wisdom

Suffering, bitter as it is, is not without meaning. Every wound hides a lesson. The lotus — the flower that is born from mud — is the perfect image of the healed soul: from the depths of pain, beauty can arise.

Our scars are not shames, but testimonies of survival. They become stories that inspire and give courage to others. A healed soul often becomes the best support for souls still in pain.

Testimony of a Healed Soul

True healing of the soul is not a process of forgetting, but an alchemical transformation. You are not defined by your wounds, but by the way you have transmuted them into light. A healed soul is not one that has never suffered, but one that has chosen not to remain a prisoner of that suffering.

A person with a healed soul emanates a different energy. They no longer seek to dominate or fight to prove their worth. They no longer need external validation, for they have found their own source of value. You see it in their eyes: fear is gone, replaced by deep peace. You feel it in their presence: a calm power, an unconditional acceptance.

Such a soul no longer judges, for it understands. It no longer reacts impulsively, for it has learned to respond with wisdom. It no longer flees from pain, but embraces it as an old teacher.

The Legacy of Healing

Healing your soul is not only a personal mission. It is a gift you bequeath to the world. Every healed soul contributes to the healing of the collective consciousness. When you release bitterness, the space around you grows brighter. When you choose love instead of hatred, a small fragment of all humanity does the same.

This process is not an act of egoism. It is, in fact, the highest form of altruism. You cannot truly give from an empty or broken vessel. But from a full vessel, the water of life flows naturally and touches others.

The Final Liberation

Ultimately, the purpose of healing is not merely to feel better. It is to be free — free from the invisible chains of the past, from the fears that held you back, from the burden of guilt and shame.

This liberation brings you closer to your essence, to the divine spark you carry within. It reminds you that you are not just a passing body and a restless mind, but an eternal being, capable of infinite love.

When the soul is fully healed, it returns home — not to a physical place, but to a state of being where separation no longer exists, where you are one with the whole. This is the state of supreme freedom: to be yourself, without mask, without fear, without judgment.

Final Reflection

Ask yourself:

– If my soul were fully healed, how would I live?

– Which chains am I ready to leave behind?

– What gifts could I offer the world from my place of healing?

We began this journey with the idea that life is a circle, and we end it with the certainty that healing transforms that circle into an ascending spiral — a spiral of evolution, wisdom, and love. And you, dear reader, are on this spiral, rising with every step you take toward the light.

Extended Conclusion

Healing is not an event, but a gentle fidelity to yourself, repeated day by day. It begins where you stop fighting what you feel and choose to be on your own side, like your dearest friend. Three simple practices can anchor this path:

1. **Conscious breathing** — a few minutes counting gentle inhales and exhales, letting the body show you that you are safe.
2. **The heart's journal** — write daily three truths you are living and three genuine thank-yous; words on paper move energy from chaos to clarity.
3. **A small act of kindness** — one concrete deed, however modest, aligned with love: a phone call, an embrace, a spoken forgiveness.

With repetition, the energy of pain loses its power to define your identity. In its place appears a spacious inner field where emotions can come and go without toppling you. In that field, faith is no longer an idea but a breath: "I am carried. I am not alone."

Do not forget the body — the temple where grace works. Nourish it simply, move it gently, rest it with respect. A healed heart dwells in a cared-for body. And when, inevitably, you fall again, remember: healing also means beginning again — every time.

The ultimate truth of healing is this: you are not seeking a "perfect" version of yourself; you are remembering who you are beneath the wounds. When you live from there, your very presence becomes balm — for you, for your loved ones, for the world.

Questions for Reflection

– What truth of mine needs to be written (not perfectly, but sincerely) so that healing can find direction?

– What small act of kindness will I make today — toward myself or someone else — as proof of my choice for healing?

NOTES

Chapter 11

Truths Beyond the Human

In this chapter I will set down a few things that, for ordinary people, may seem hard to believe. I do not write them to impress, but so that you may learn the truth and open your mind to the limitless.

In another life I created another planet, at a very great distance from Earth. There I brought into existence beings similar to humans, yet in a continual evolution of goodness. That planet still exists today. The appearance of its inhabitants is identical to that of humans, but they live eternally, need neither to reproduce nor to eat. They can become spirit at any time and can teleport.

I also created another dimension in which I placed beings akin to humans — beings of a spiritual nature. At one point, they began to fight among themselves. Then I intervened, making it so that whenever they looked at one another, they recognized in the one before them their own self. In that instant, the fighting ceased. That dimension and those beings still exist.

On Earth, things are the same: all of us are One, manifested in countless forms. From the atomic level to the most unusual beings — humans, animals, birds, fish, insects, and other creatures — the same Consciousness expresses itself in different ways. We are in them, and they are in us. We are a single Spirit manifesting across all planes of existence.

Some people, because they have had access to secret information or belong to hidden groups, consider themselves superior to ordinary people and look down on them. They do not know they will return to Earth in other bodies and will meet their own thoughts and deeds. I have lived many times on Earth and reached the highest levels in human terms. I was part of the most important group of people on the planet, and I lived, in turn, the life of each member of that group, because Earth has been "restarted" many times.

Those who are "on top" today do not know they will not remain there forever, but that someone else will come into the body they now inhabit. Earth will reset again, and their spirit will inhabit other bodies. I have had many lives in which I belonged to groups with access to secret information. My mistake — and the mistake of those today — was that we were caught in an illusory light from which we looked with contempt upon simple people. I do not judge anyone, for I too have been like that.

What I wish to explain is that people do not perceive that frequency which gathers all that has life; like a conveyor belt, it collects everything, including those who believe themselves invincible. Then everything "restarts," everything begins again and repeats: the Spanish flu, the First World War, the Second World War — all repeat, yet each of us is in a different physical body.

I am convinced that few people on the planet understand and know these things. My message for those "on top" is this: do now what you would wish to meet later. When I was on top, no one told me these truths. You who are on top have the opportunity to change what will happen in the next cycle when Earth, with all that is on it, repeats. You will meet what you have changed — only you will be in other bodies. If you wish to meet goodness, you must do good.

This message is for every human being. Each will meet what they have done, whether spirit, entity, human, "extraterrestrial," and so on. Regardless of the form of manifestation, every being will meet its own manifestations — both thoughts and deeds.

In closing, I wish all people to be wise and choose the good. If someone cannot, for the moment, do good, it is better to do no harm to anyone, for the harm you do to another you in fact do to yourself and prepare it for your own future.

Be wise!

Conclusion

Truths beyond the human are not meant to bring fear, but light. They show us that nothing is random, that every life has a purpose, and that every choice leaves a trace in the fabric of the universe. Though it seems we are separated by bodies, by social roles, by different eras, in reality we are expressions of the same eternal Spirit.

What we do today is not lost in the void; it will return to us in other forms, in other times. Therefore the responsibility we bear for our thoughts and deeds is immense. They shape not only the present, but our future and the future of those beside us.

The message for those "on top," and for each of us, is simple: your deeds today become your world tomorrow. The power you hold is not an eternal privilege, but a test. If you use it for good, you will reap good. If you use it for harm or indifference, you will meet the very shadows you have created.

True wisdom does not lie in hoarding secret information or climbing the rungs of worldly hierarchy, but in recognizing that all is One. Every gesture, however small, has a cosmic echo. By choosing to do good, even when it seems not to matter, you are in fact choosing for your eternity.

In the end, the lesson is this: freedom does not mean escaping the cycle of life, but creating consciously — with love — within it.

Questions for Reflection

– If everything repeats and I will meet my deeds again, what do I choose to create today?

– How can I transform the power I have — however small — into an instrument of good?

NOTES

Epilogue

The Journey of the Soul and the Return to Love

This book has not been just a collection of words, but a journey — a bridge between past and future, between the visible and the invisible, between human fragility and the eternity of the soul. Each chapter has been a step, a window toward truths that the soul has always known, but that the mind forgets.

I have spoken of past lives, of power and love, of the repeated lessons of existence and of the healing that awaits us when we choose to look into the heart. I have touched mysteries and revealed fragments of realities greater than those we perceive with the naked eye. But beyond all this, the most important reminder is a simple one: we are One.

There is no true separation between people, between worlds, between times. Everything you have lived, everything you will live, every smile and every tear, every victory and every fall — all are part of the same sacred dance of the Spirit discovering itself.

This book does not ask you to believe, but to feel. To listen to the quiet voice of your soul and to remember who you are: a divine spark, eternal, part of an infinite whole.

A Message for You, Dear Reader

Thank you for coming this far, for choosing to open your heart and to read these pages with an awakened soul.

I want you to know a truth both simple and deep: you are loved. Not for what you do, not for what you have, not for who you think you "must" be, but for who you are in your essence — a child of Light, pure and radiant.

No matter how heavy your path has been, no matter how many wounds you have carried, no matter how deep the shadows — they do not define who you are. They have only been teachers. Your true identity is love.

Live with gentleness. Forgive yourself and forgive others. Rejoice in simple things. Choose to do good even when no one sees. In every act of love, in every moment of compassion, you illuminate the whole world.

And when you forget, remember: you are not alone. We are together, beyond time, beyond veils. We are One.

This book is not just a gathering of words.

It is a calling, a thread of light handed to you so that you may remember who you truly are.

Every page is a mirror. What you read here is not only my story, but also yours. You will find fragments of your own path, you will feel the echo of your own soul, and perhaps you will hear the secret voice of your heart whispering:

"You are more than your body."
"You are never alone."
"You are love, and love is all that remains."

I offer you these lines with the hope that they will bring you peace, courage, and trust in your own light.

Wherever you may be along the way, do not forget: you are a gift to this world.

And the whole world is richer simply because you exist.

Be light. Be love. Be free.

With love and gratitude,
Sandor Onisim Bereczki

www.ingramcontent.com/pod-product-compliance
Lightning Source LLC
Chambersburg PA
CBHW022213090526
44584CB00013BA/840